MW00511295

Air Fryer Cookbook

Top 60 Air Fryer Recipes with Low Salt, Low Fat and Less Oil.

Amazingly Easy Recipes to Fry, Bake, Grill, and Roast with Your Air Fryer

Ronda Williams

Table of Contents

Introduction

What is Air Frying?

First, a quick explanation of what air frying is and isn't. They don't fry food at all. They are more like a self-contained convection oven than a deep fat fryer. Most units have one or more heating elements, along with a fan or two to circulate the hot air. These appliances quickly heat and circulate the hot air around and through the food in the tray. This cooking method takes advantage of the heat and the drying effect of the air to cook foods quickly, leaving them crisp and browned on the outside but still moist inside. While the results can be similar to using a deep fryer, they are not identical.

What Are The Pros And Cons Of An Air Fryer?

While the enthusiasm about these products may be a bit overblown, there are some solid benefits to using an air fryer, as well as some major downsides.

Pros Of An Air Fryer

1. Healthier Meals

You do not need to use much (or any) oil in these appliances to get your food crispy and browned! Most users just spritz a little oil on the item and then proceed to the cooking cycle. The hot air takes advantage of the little bit of oil, and any excess oil just drains away from the food. This makes these devices ideal for making fresh and frozen fries, onion rings, mozzarella sticks, chicken wings, and nuggets. Unlike a traditional oven, air frying items are cooked faster and the excess oil doesn't soak into your food. So the claims that they use less oil and make healthier meals are true!

2. Quicker, More Efficient Cooking

Air fryers take just minutes to preheat, and most of the heat stays inside the appliance. Foods cook faster than in an oven or on a stovetop because this heat is not lost to the surrounding air. Even frozen foods are quickly cooked because the effect of the heat is intensified by the circulating air. These units are also more energy-efficient than an oven. Using a fryer will not heat your house in the summer, and the cost of the electricity used is just pennies. Since the cooking cycle is also shorter, you can see that using a fryer makes most cooking faster and more efficient than traditional appliances!

3. Versatility

You can use them to air fry, stir fry, reheat, bake, broil, roast, grill, steam, and even rotisserie in some models. Besides the fries and nuggets, you can make hot dogs and sausages, steak, chicken breasts or thighs, grilled sandwiches, stir-fried meats and veggies, roasted or steamed veggies, all kinds of fish and shrimp dishes, even cakes and desserts. If your unit is large enough, you can even bake a whole chicken or small turkey, or do a beef or pork roast. They are more than just a fryer!

4. Space-Saving

Most units are about the size of a coffee maker. Some models are small and super-compact, making them perfect for small kitchens, kitchenettes, dorm rooms, or RVs. An air fryer can replace an oven in a situation that lacks one and can be more useful than a toaster oven or steamer. If you use it frequently you will likely be happy to give it a home on your kitchen counter!

5. Easy To Use

Most fryers are designed to be easy to use. Just set the cooking temperature and time, put your food in the basket, and walk away. Of course, you will get better results if you shake your food once or twice during the cooking cycle, especially for things like fries, chips, wings, and nuggets. This ensures even browning and perfect results. Many air fryer enthusiasts have even taught their children to use them for making after school snacks or quick lunches!

Cons of an Air Fryer

1. Quality Issues

Air fryers are mostly made from plastic and inexpensive metal parts. They may or may not bear up after months or years of use. The heating elements, controls, and fans tend to go out eventually, and once they do your unit is useless. The metal cooking baskets and pans do not tend to last very long and often need to be replaced. Print on the dials or control panels can wear off. Even expensive units can have these issues, and some brands seem to have a lot of reported problems. These are not sturdy, long-lasting kitchen appliances overall.

2. Takes Up Space

Ok, I had "Space Saver" listed as a pro...how can it be a con as well? Easy! They do take up space, either on your counter or stored away in a cabinet. If you use it frequently this might not be a problem...but if you only drag it out to make the occasional batch of wings then the loss of space might not make it worth it to you. It depends on how and if you use it. Some units are fairly heavy as well, and might not be very easy to move around. They have the potential to be just another appliance you use a few times and then sell at a yard sale.

3. Not Ideal For Large Families

You will see some fryers advertised for "large families" but what does that mean? Most air fryers are best suited to making food for 1-4 people (depending on the capacity). There are very few that can handle making food for more than 4, and they often still require cooking in batches. For large families, a true convection air frying oven would probably be a better choice.

A medium-sized fryer with a capacity of 3.5 quarts can usually handle the main dish for two or a main and side dish for one. A large unit with a capacity of 5.8 quarts can handle the main dish like a whole chicken...which theoretically means enough to serve 4 people, as long as you cook the rest of the food in another appliance. So these are ideal for smaller families or single users, or a dorm or office snack maker.

4. Learning Curve

They ARE easy to use, but there is still a learning curve. Each unit has its peculiarities that you will have to figure out. They come with cooking guides and recipes, but those are more recommendations rather than firm instructions. It may take a few trials before you get the results that you want. Luckily the internet is filled with users who have shared their experiences, so finding tips is pretty easy.

5. Limitations

For all their versatility, air fryers have limitations as well. You are limited by the size and shape of the basket. Your frozen taquitos may not fit into some models, and you might be limited to a 6-inch pie pan in another. Food sometimes gets stuck to the cooking pans, meaning a more difficult clean-up for you. Even with accessories like elevated cooking racks and kabob skewers, you will still have to cook in batches or use another appliance if you are making food for multiple people. You also have to wait for the unit to cool off before cleaning and storing it away. For some people, these limitations might be too much to make an air fryer worth it.

Air Fryer Benefits

- An air fryer has many benefits to offer its customers.
- Low-fat meals
- Easy cleanup
- Uses hot-air circulation, the air fryer cooks your ingredients from all angles- with no oil needed.
- This ultimately produces healthier foods than most fryers and spares you from that unwanted aroma of fried foods in your home.
- To make sure you get the most out of your appliance, most fryers are accompanied by a recipe book to help you get started right away on your journey of fast, yet healthy meal preparations.

- Whether your favorite dish is french fries, muffins, chips, chicken tenders, or grilled vegetables, an air fryer can prepare it all.

Is an Air Fryer Useful?

At the tip of your fingers, you can have an appliance that specializes in making delicious, healthy meals that look and taste just like the ones made in oil fryers. The air fryer serves up many ways to be useful in your life.

Consider:

- Do you find yourself short on time to cook?
- Are you having a hard time letting go of those fatty foods, but still want to lose weight?
- Are you always seeking to get a bang for your buck?

If you answered yes to any of these questions, then an air fryer may be for you.

Why You Should Use An Air Fryer

An air fryer can pretty much do it all. And by all, we mean fry, grill, bake, and roast. Equipped with sturdy plastic and metal material, the air fryer has many great benefits to offer.

Air Fryers Can:

- Cook multiple dishes at once
- Cut back on fatty oils
- Prepare a meal within minutes
- While every appliance has its cons, the air fryer doesn't offer many.
- The fryer may be bulky in weight, but its dimensions are slimmer than most fryers. An air fryer can barely take up any counter space.
- If you need fast, healthy, convenient, and tasty, then once again, an air fryer may be for you.

Air Fryer- Healthier

The biggest quality the air fryer offers is healthier dishes

In comparison to other fryers, air fryers were designed to specifically function without fattening oils and to produce food with up to 80 percent less fat than food cooked with other fryers. The air fryer can help you lose the weight, you've been dying to get rid of. While it can be difficult to let go of your favorite fried foods, an air fryer will let you have your cake and eat it too. You can still have your fried dishes, but at the same time, still conserve those calories and saturated fat. The air fryer can also grill, bake, and roast foods as well. Offering you an all in one combination, the air fryer is the perfect appliance for anyone looking to switch to a healthier lifestyle.

Fast And Quick

- If you're on a tight schedule, you may want to use an air fryer.
- Within minutes you can have crunchy golden fries or crispy chicken tenders.
- This fryer is perfect for people who are constantly on the go and do not have much time to prepare meals.
- With most air fryers, french fries can be prepared within 12 minutes.
- That cuts the time you spend in the kitchen by a tremendous amount.

Features

1. Temperature And Timer

- Avoid the waiting time for your fryer to decide when it wants to heat up.
- With an air fryer, once you power it on, the fryer will instantly heat.
- When using the appliance cold, that is, right after it has been off for a while (since last use) all you have to do is add three minutes to your cooking time to allow for it to heat up properly.
- The appliance is equipped with adjustable temperature control that allows you to set the temperature that can be altered for each of your

meals.

- Most fryers can go up to 200-300 degrees.
- Because the fryer can cook food at record times, it comes with a timer that can be pre-set with no more than 30 minutes.
- You can even check on the progress of your foods without messing up the set time. Simply pull out the pan, and the fryer will cause heating. When you replace the pan, heating will resume.
- When your meal is prepared and your timer runs out, the fryer will alert you with its ready sound indicator. But just in-case you can't make it to the fryer when the timer goes, the fryer will automatically switch off to help prevent your ingredients from overcooking and burning.

2. Food Separator

Some air fryers are supplied with a food separator that enables you to prepare multiple meals at once. For example, if you wanted to prepare frozen chicken nuggets and french fries, you could use the separator to cook both ingredients at the same time, all the while avoiding the worry of the flavors mixing. An air fryer is perfect for quick and easy, lunch and dinner combinations. It is recommended to pair similar ingredients together when using the separator. This will allow both foods to share a similar temperature setting.

3. Air Filter

Some air fryers are built with an integrated air filter that eliminates those unwanted vapors and food odors from spreading around your house. No more smelling like your favorite fried foods, the air filter will diffuse that hot oil steam that floats and sticks. You can now enjoy your fresh kitchen smell before, during, and after using your air fryer.

4. Cleaning

- No need to fret after using an air fryer, it was designed for hassle-free cleaning.
- The parts of the fryer are constructed of non-stick material.
- This prevents any food from sticking to surfaces that ultimately make

it hard to clean.
- It is recommended to soak the parts of the appliances before cleaning.
- All parts such as the grill, pan, and basket are removable and dishwasher friendly.
- After your ingredients are cooked to perfection, you can simply place your parts in the dishwasher for a quick and easy clean.

Tips on Cleaning an Air Fryer:

- Use detergent that specializes in dissolving oil.
- For a maximum and quick cleaning, leave the pan to soak in water and detergent for a few minutes.
- Avoid using metal utensils when cleaning the appliance to prevent scuffs and scratches on the material.
- Always let the fryer cool off for about 30 minutes before you wash it.

5. Cost-effective

Are there any cost-effective air fryers? For all that they can do, air fryers can be worth the cost. It has been highly questionable if the benefits of an air fryer are worth the expense. When you weigh your pros and cons, the air fryer surely leads with its pros. There aren't many fryers on the market that can fry, bake, grill and roast; and also promise you healthier meals. An air fryer saves you time, and could potentially save you money. Whether the air fryer is cost-effective for your life, is ultimately up to you.

The air fryer is a highly recommendable appliance to anyone starting a new diet, parents with busy schedules, or individuals who are always on the go. Deciding whether the investment is worth it, is all up to the purchaser. By weighing the air fryer advantages and the unique differences the air fryer has, compared to other fryers, you should be able to decide whether the air fryer has a lot to bring to the table.

Breakfast Recipes

1. Delicious Breakfast Potatoes

Preparation time: 10 minutes Cooking time: 35 minutes

Ingredients:

- 2 tablespoons olive oil
- 3 potatoes, cubed
- 1 yellow onion, chopped
- 1 red bell pepper, chopped
- Salt and black pepper to the taste
- 1 teaspoon garlic powder
- 1 teaspoon sweet paprika
- 1 teaspoon onion powder

Instructions:

- Grease your air fryer's basket with olive oil, add potatoes, toss and season with salt and pepper.
- Add onion, bell pepper, garlic powder, paprika and onion powder, toss well, cover and cook at 370 degrees F for 30 minutes.
- Divide potatoes mix on plates and serve for breakfast.

Nutrition Facts:

calories 214, fat 6, fiber 8, carbs 15, protein 4

2. Breakfast Sandwich

Prep Time: 10 minutes

Ingredients

- 1 egg
- 1 English muffin
- 2 slices of bacon
- Salt and pepper, to taste

Instructions

- Preheat the air fryer to 395 degrees. Crack the egg into a ramekin. Place the muffin, egg and bacon in the air fryer.
- Cook for 6 minutes. Let cool slightly so you can assemble the sandwich.
- Cut the muffin in half. Place the egg on one half and season with salt and pepper.
- Arrange the bacon on top. Top with the other muffin half.

Nutrition Facts

Calories 240.7, Carbohydrates 25.5 g, Fat 8.8 g, Protein 13.3 g

3. Prosciutto, Mozzarella and Egg in a Cup

Prep Time: 20 minutes

Ingredients

- 2 slices of bread
- 2 prosciutto slices, chopped
- 2 eggs
- 4 tomato slices ¼ tsp. balsamic vinegar
- 2 tbsp. grated mozzarella ¼ tsp. maple syrup
- 2 tbsp. mayonnaise
- Salt and pepper, to taste

Instructions

- Preheat the air fryer to 320 degrees. grease two large ramekins. Place one bread slice in the bottom of each ramekin.
- Arrange 2 tomato slices on top of each bread slice. Divide the mozzarella between the ramekins.
- Crack the eggs over the mozzarella
- .Drizzle with maple syrup and balsamic vinegar. Season with some salt and pepper.
- Cook for 10 minutes, or until desired.

Nutrition Facts

Calories 291.3, Carbohydrates 12.9 g, Fat 20.5 g, Protein 13 g

4. Air Fried Shirred Eggs

Prep Time: 20 minutes

Ingredients

- 2 tsp. butter, for greasing
- 4 eggs, divided
- 2 tbsp. heavy cream4 slices of ham
- 3 tbsp. Parmesan cheese
- ¼ tsp. paprika
- ¾ tsp. salt
- ¼ tsp. pepper
- 2 tsp. chopped chives

Instructions

- Preheat the air fryer to 320 degrees F.grease a pie pan with the butter.
- Arrange the ham slices on the bottom of the pan to cover it completely.Use more slices if needed (or less if your pan is smaller).
- Whisk one egg along with the heavy cream, salt and pepper, in a small bowl.Pour the mixture over the ham slices.Crack the other eggs over the ham.
- Sprinkle the Parmesan cheese.
- Cook for 14 minutes.Sprinkle with paprika and garnish with chives.Serve with bread.

Nutrition Facts

279.9, Carbohydrates 1.8 g, Fat 20 g, Protein 20.8 g

5. Very Berry Breakfast Puff

Prep Time: 20 Minutes

Ingredients

- 3 pastry dough sheets

- 2 tbsp. mashed strawberries
- 2 tbsp. mashed raspberries
- ¼ tsp. vanilla extract2 cups cream cheese1 tbsp. honey

Instructions

- Preheat the air fryer to 375 degrees F.Divide the cream cheese between the dough sheets and spread it evenly.In a small bowl combine the berries, honey and vanilla.
- Divide the mixture between the pastry sheets.Pinch the ends of the sheets, to form puff.
- You can seal them by brushing some water onto the edges, or even better, use egg wash. Place the puffs on a lined baking dish.Place in the air fryer and cook for 15 minutes

Nutrition Facts

Calories 255.9, Carbohydrates 24.5 g, Fat 15.7 g, Protein 4.3

6. <u>Cheese Air Fried Bake</u>

Preparation time: 10 minutes Cooking time: 20 minutes

Ingredients:

- 4 bacon slices, cooked and crumbled
- 2 cups milk
- 2 and ½ cups cheddar cheese, shredded
- 1 pound breakfast sausage, casings removed and chopped
- 2 eggs
- ½ teaspoon onion powder
- Salt and black pepper to the taste
- 3 tablespoons parsley, chopped
- Cooking spray

Instructions:

In a bowl, mix eggs with milk, cheese, onion powder, salt, pepper and parsley and whisk well.

grease your air fryer with cooking spray, heat it up at 320 degrees F and add bacon and sausage.

Add eggs mix, spread and cook for 20 minutes.

Divide among plates and serve.

Nutrition Facts:

calories 214, fat 5, fiber 8, carbs 12, protein 12

Main & Lunch Recipes

7. <u>Air Fried Calzone</u>

Prep Time: 20 minutes

Ingredients

- Pizza dough, preferably homemade
- 4 oz. cheddar cheese, grated
- 1 oz. mozzarella cheese
- 1 oz. bacon, diced
- 2 cups cooked and shredded turkey (leftovers are fine)1 egg, beaten
- 1 tsp. thyme4 tbsp. tomato paste1 tsp. basil
- 1 tsp. oreganoSalt and pepper, to taste

Instructions

- Preheat the air fryer to 350 degrees F.Divide the pizza dough into 4 equal pieces so you have dough for 4 small pizza crusts.
- Combine the tomato paste, basil, oregano, and thyme, in a small bowl.
- Brush the mixture onto the crusts just make sure not to go all the way and avoid brushing near the edges.
- On one half of each crust, place ½ turkey, and season the meat with some salt and pepper.
- Top the meat with some bacon.
- Combine the cheddar and mozzarella and divide it between the pizzas, making sure that you layer only one half of the dough.
- Brush the edges of the crust with the beaten egg.
- Fold the crust and seal with a fork.Cook for 10 minutes

Nutrition Facts

Calories 339, Carbohydrates 10.6 g, Fat 17.3 g, Protein 33.6 g

8. Roasted Radish and Onion Cheesy Salad

Prep Time: 35 minute

Ingredients

1 lb. radishes, green parts too

- 1 large red onion, sliced
- ½ lb. mozzarella, sliced
- 2 tbsp. olive oil, plus more for drizzling
- 2 tbsp. balsamic glaze
- 1 tsp. dried basil
- 1 tsp. dried parsley
- 1 tsp. salt

Instructions

- Preheat the air fryer to 350 degrees F. Wash the radishes well and dry them by patting with paper towels.
- Cut them in half and place in a large bowl. Add the onion slices in.
- Stir in salt, basil, parsley and olive oil. Place in the basket of the air fryer.
- Cook for 30 minutes.
- Make sure to toss them twice while cooking. Stir in the mozzarella immediately so that it begins to melt. Stir in the balsamic glaze. Drizzle with olive oil

Nutrition Facts

Calories 240.1, Carbohydrates 9.7 g, Fat 16 g, Protein 15

9. <u>Mock Stir Fry</u>

Prep Time: 25 minutes

Ingredients

- 4 boneless and skinless chicken breasts cut into cubes
- 2 carrots, sliced
- 1 red bell pepper, cut into strips
- 1 yellow bell pepper, cut into strips
- 1 cup snow peas
- 15 oz. broccoli florets
- 1 scallion, slicedSauce:
- 3 tbsp. soy sauce
- 2 tbsp. oyster sauce
- 1 tbsp. brown sugar
- 1 tsp. sesame oil1 tsp. cornstarch
- 1 tsp. sriracha
- 2 garlic cloves, minced1 tbsp. grated ginger
- 1 tbsp. rice wine vinegar

Instructions

- Preheat the air fryer to 370 degrees F.
- Place the chicken, bell peppers, and carrot, in a bowl. In a small bowl, combine the sauce **Ingredients**.
- Coat the chicken mixture with the sauce. Place on a lined baking sheet and cook for 5 minutes.
- Add snow peas and broccoli and cook for additional 8 to10 minutes. Serve garnished with scallion

Nutrition Facts

Calories 277, Carbohydrates 15.6 g, Fat 4.4 g, Protein 43.1 g

10. **Potato and Bacon Salad**

Prep Time: 10 minutes

Ingredients

- 4 lb. boiled and cubed potatoes
- 15 bacon slices, chopped
- 2 cups shredded cheddar cheese
- 15 oz. sour cream
- 2 tbsp. mayonnaise
- 1 tsp. salt
- 1 tsp. pepper
- 1 tsp. dried herbs by choice

Instructions

- Preheat the air fryer to 350 degrees F.
- Combine the potatoes, bacon, salt, pepper, and herbs, in a large bowl.
- Transfer to a baking dish. Cook for about 7 minutes.
- Stir in sour cream and mayonnaise.

Nutrition Facts

Calories 306.5, Carbohydrates 33.9 g, Fat 14.9 g, Protein 10 g

11.   Carbonara and Mushroom Spaghetti

Prep Time: 30 - 35 minutes

Ingredients

- ½ lb. white button mushrooms, sliced
- ½ cup of water
- 1 tsp. butter
- 2 garlic cloves, chopped
- 12 oz. spaghetti, cooked
- 14 oz. carbonara mushroom sauce (store bought)Salt and pepper, to taste

Instructions

- Preheat the air fryer to 300 degrees F.
- Add the butter and garlic and cook for 3 minutes.
- Add the mushrooms and cook for 5 more minutes.
- Stir in mushroom carbonara sauce and water.
- Season with salt and pepper.
- Cook for 18 minutes. Stir in the spaghetti and cook for 1 minute more.

Nutrition Facts

Calories 395.7, Carbohydrates 57.9 g, Fat 13 g, Protein 13 g

Side Dishes & Dinner Recipes

12.   <u>Air Fryer Mushrooms</u>

Prep Time: 5 minutes

Cook Time: 15 minutes

Ingredients

- 7 oz 200 grams chestnut mushrooms
- 2 tsp vegetable oil
- 2 tsp low sodium soy sauce or tamari sauce
- 1 sprig rosemary
- ½ tsp salt and pepper

Instructions

- Cut the mushrooms into thick slices, I usually cut each into 2 halves but if it's too big then I cut into smaller pieces. Try to make the size of the slices even so everything cooks evenly.
- In a white bowl, toss the mushrooms with the rest of the ingredients so everything is well coated in soy, oil, and seasonings.
- No need to preheat the Air Fryer. Place the mushrooms directly into the Air Fryer basket, and cook at 356f (180) for about 15 minutes flipping halfway through.
- Open the Air Fryer basket and check every 5 minutes, shake the basket and decide how much longer you would like to cook the mushrooms for.
- The mushrooms should be cooked well, but not dried out or burnt. So make sure not to overcook them.
- Serve with some extra sea salt flakes, and red chili flakes if desired.

Nutrition

- Calories: 30kcal | Carbohydrates: 2g | Protein: 1g | Fat: 2g | Saturated Fat: 1g | Sodium: 377mg | Potassium: 222mg | Fiber: 1g | Sugar: 1g | Calcium: 9mg | Iron: 1mg

13.   Easy Air Fryer Baked Potatoes

Prep Time: 5 minutes

Cook Time: 35 minutes

Total Time: 40 minutes

Ingredients

- 4 medium russet potatoes scrubbed and dried
- 4 teaspoons olive oil
- 1 teaspoon kosher sea salt plus more for serving if desired

Instructions

- Preheat the air fryer to 375°F for about 10 minutes.
- Wash, dry, and prick each potato
- Drizzle each potato with oil and sprinkle with salt.
- Place 2 to 4 potatoes in your air fryer, depending on size.
- Set air fryer to cook at 375° for 35 minutes, or until potatoes are fork-tender.
- Use tongs to remove potatoes from the air fryer basket then carefully cut a slit in the top of each one.
- Add desired toppings & enjoy!

Nutrition

- Serving: 1g | Calories: 204kcal | Carbohydrates: 38g | Protein: 5g | Fat: 4g | Saturated Fat: 1g | Sodium: 592mg | Potassium: 888mg | Fiber: 3g | Sugar: 1g | Vitamin C: 12mg | Calcium: 28mg | Iron: 2mg

14. Crispy Spicy Air Fryer Okra

Prep Time: 10 Minutes

Cook Time: 10 Minutes

Total Time: 20 Minutes

Ingredients

- 1 1/4 lb fresh okra
- For the egg wash:
- 1 egg
- 1/2 tsp coriander
- 1/2 tsp smoked paprika
- 1/2 tsp chili powder (optional)
- Pinch of salt
- For the panko breading:
- 1 cup gluten-free flaked panko breading
- 1 tsp coriander
- 1 tsp smoked paprika
- 1/2 tsp chili powder (optional)
- 1/2 tsp garlic powder
- 2 tbsp parsley
- 1/4 tsp each salt and pepper

Instructions

- Rinse okra and dry thoroughly - I used paper towels to do so.
- Prepare egg wash by mixing the egg with coriander, smoked paprika, chili powder (if using), and salt in a bowl.
- Prepare to bread by mixing panko bread flakes with coriander, smoked paprika, chili powder (if using), garlic powder, parsley, salt, and pepper.
- Then, using one hand, dip the dried okra in the spiced egg wash and drop it onto the plate with the breading.
- Then, using the other hand, coat the okra well with the spiced panko breading. Repeat this with all the okra.

27

- When the okra is all breaded, place them in a single layer at the bottom of your air fryer basket and spray them with your favorite cooking spray.
- For best results, preheat the air fryer to 400 degrees for 2-3 minutes.
- Set the air fryer to air fry the okra at 400 degrees for 4-5 minutes. Then open the air fryer, and using tongs, flip the okra over and air fry for 4-5 minutes at 400 degrees. Repeat if you have any more breaded okra (depending on the size of your air fryer, this might take 2-3 batches to cook - but the result works it.
- Enjoy with your favorite sauces!

Nutrition Information

- Calories: 150
- Total Fat: 3g
- Saturated Fat: 1g
- Trans Fat: 0g
- Unsaturated Fat: 2g
- Cholesterol: 66mg
- Sodium: 302mg
- Carbohydrates: 23g
- Fiber: 4g
- Sugar: 4g
- Protein: 8g

15. <u>Air Fryer Radishes (Healthy Side Dish)</u>

Prep Time: 10 minutes

Cook Time: 15 minutes

Total Time: 25 minutes

Ingredients

- 1 pound (or 454 gram packages) fresh radishes or about 3 cups halved
- 1 tablespoon extra virgin olive oil
- 1/2 teaspoon dried oregano
- 1/2 teaspoon kosher salt
- 1/4 teaspoon garlic powder
- 1/4 teaspoon onion powder
- Dash of ground black pepper

Instructions

- Wash and trim the radishes, scrubbing off any dirt and cutting off any dark spots. Pat dry with a paper towel.
- Slice the radishes in half so they are roughly 1-inch pieces (it doesn't need to be exact), or quarter them if they are larger.
- Place the radishes in a large bowl and evenly coat with oil. Add the seasonings and toss to combine.
- Place radishes in the air fryer basket and air fry on 400F for 15-17 minutes, or until fork-tender. Shake or stir the radishes after about 10 minutes. Serve immediately.

Nutritional Facts

- Calories: 48
- Total Fat: 3.6g
- Total Carbohydrate: 3.4g
- Sugar: 0g
- Calcium: 33.7mg
- Sat Fat: 0.5g
- Sodium: 373.4mg

- Fiber: 1.7g
- Protein: 1.3g
- Vitamin C: 32.9mg
- Iron: 1mg

16. **Air Fryer Zucchini And Onions**

Total Time: 30 mins

Ingredients

- 2-3 zucchini small-medium sized
- 1 red onion
- 2 tbsp olive oil or avocado oil
- 1/2 tsp dried basil
- 1/2 tsp salt
- 1/2 tsp dried oregano
- 1/2 tsp garlic powder
- 1/4 tsp black pepper

Instructions

- Do the Prep Work
- Preheat your Air Fryer to 400F.
- Meanwhile, wash and dice the zucchini and onions, at least twice the size of the holes in your air fryer basket.
- In a bowl, toss the vegetables, oil, and all the Italian seasonings together.
- Cook the Dish
- Pour the vegetable mixture into the heated air fryer, then shake or spread the vegetables so they're evenly spaced out in the basket. Close and set the timer for 20 minutes.
- Halfway through cook time, open the air fryer and shake the basket or turn the vegetables with a spoon or spatula. Close and allow to finish cooking, then season to taste if needed and serve. Note: Sometime in the final two to three minutes, open the air fryer to make sure the vegetables aren't beginning to burn.

Nutrition

- Calories: 91kcal | Carbohydrates: 6g | Protein: 2g | Fat: 7g | Saturated Fat: 1g | Sodium: 300mg | Potassium: 296mg | Fiber: 1g | Sugar: 4g | Vitamin A: 196IU | Vitamin C: 20mg | Calcium: 25mg | Iron: 1mg

31

17.   <u>Air Fryer Baby Potatoes (Easy Side Dish)</u>

Prep Time: 5 minutes

Cook Time: 18 minutes

Total Time: 23 minutes

Ingredients

- 4 cups baby potatoes, skin on, pre-washed, and halved
- 1 lime, juiced
- 1 tablespoon extra virgin olive oil
- 1 tablespoon chili powder
- 1/2 teaspoon sea salt

Instructions

- Place potatoes in a large bowl and coat them with lime juice. Drain any excess juice.
- Add the oil, chili powder, and sea salt and stir until potatoes are well coated.
- Arrange the potatoes in a single layer in the air fryer basket. Roast on 400F for 15-18 minutes, or until the potatoes are tender with crispy edges. You can check on them after 7-8 minutes and give them a shake or stir.
- Serve immediately (while hot and crispy).

Nutritional Facts

- Calories: 95
- Total Fat: 2.6g
- Total Carbohydrate: 17g
- Sugar: 1.4g
- Calcium: 14.6mg
- Sat Fat: 0.4g
- Sodium: 248.6mg
- Fiber: 1.7g
- Protein: 1.9g

Snacks And Appetizers

18. <u>Air Fried Shrimp Tails</u>

Prep Time: 15 mins

Total Time: 20 mins

Ingredients

1 lb of peeled and deveined raw Shrimp

1 Cup of almond flour

1 tbsp of pepper to taste

1 tbsp of salt

1 tsp of cayenne pepper

1 tsp of cumin

1 tsp of garlic powder

1 tbsp of paprika

1 tbsp of onion powder

Instructions:

Preheat your Air Fryer to a temperature of 390° F

Peel the shrimp and devein it

Dip in the shrimp into the heavy cream

Dredge the shrimp into the mixture of the almond flour

Shake off any excess of flour

Put the shrimp in the Air Fryer basket and

Lock the lid of your Air Fryer and set the timer to about 15 minutes and the temperature to 200° C/400° F

You can check your appetizer after about 6 minutes and you can flip the shrimp if needed

When the timer beeps; turn off your Air Fryer

Serve and enjoy your shrimps!

Nutrition facts:

Calories 335

Total Fats 15.8 g

Carbs: 2.2 g

Protein 46 g

Sugar 0.2 g

Fiber 0.5 g

19. **Air fried Radish with Coconut Oil**

Prep Time: 12 mins

Total Time: 15 mins

Ingredients

- 16 Ounces of fresh radishes
- 2 tbsp of melted coconut oil
- ½ tsp of sea salt
- ½ tsp of pepper

Instructions:

Preheat your Air Fryer to a temperature of about 400 degrees F.

Slice the radishes into thin slices

Place the radish slices in a bowl and toss it with oil

Lay the radishes in the Air Fryer basket

Whisk the pepper and the salt together; then sprinkle it over the radishes

Lock the lid of your Air Fryer and set the timer for about 12 minutes

Set the temperature to about 200° C/400° F

When the timer beeps; turn off your Air Fryer

Remove the pan from the air fryer

Serve and enjoy your air fried radishes!

Nutritional info per serving:

Calories 148

Total Fats 14 g

Carbs: 6 g

Protein 3 g

Sugar 1 g

Fiber 3 g

20. Air fried Okra with Parmesan Cheese

Prep Time: 25 mins

Total Time: 10 mins

Ingredients

- 1 Pound of fresh okra
- 1 tsp of sea salt
- 2 tbsp of almond flour
- ¼ Cup of finely grated Parmesan cheese
- ½ tsp of pepper
- 1 Pinch of sea salt

Instructions:

Preheat your Air Fryer to a temperature of about 390° F

Wash the okra; then chop it into small pieces

Toss the chopped okra with the salt and a little bit of ground pepper; then set it aside for about 3 minutes

In a bowl; mix the almond flour with Parmesan cheese, the pepper, and the salt

Coat the okra pieces into the mixture and place it in your Air Fryer basket

Lock the lid and set the timer to about 25 minutes and the temperature to 390° F

When the timer beeps; turn off your Air Fryer

Remove the pan; then serve and enjoy your okras!

Nutrition facts:

Calories 42

Total Fats 1 g

Carbs: 4 g

Protein 2 g

Sugar 0.1 g

Fiber 2 g

21.   Chicken Nuggets with Almond Flour

Prep Time: 15 mins

Total Time: 18 mins

Ingredients

- 1 Whisked egg
- 4 tbsp of oil
- 2 lbs of chicken breast
- 1 Cup of almond flour
- ½ tsp of salt
- ½ tsp of garlic powder
- 1 tsp of onion flakes

Instructions

Combine the egg and the oil and whisk very well

In a separate bowl; combine the almond flour, the salt, the garlic and the onion

Cut the chicken breast meat into thin strips; then dip each of the strips into the egg mixture and coat very well

Arrange the chicken nuggets in the Air Fryer basket and spray with a little bit of oil

Lock the lid of the Air Fryer and set the timer for about 15 minutes and set the temperature for about 180° C/350° F

When the timer beeps; turn off your Air Fryer

Serve and enjoy the chicken nuggets!

Nutrition facts:

Calories 170.1

Total Fats 9.2 g

Carbs: 13 g

Protein 11 g

Sugar 5 g

Fiber 1 g

22. Easy Crab Sticks

Preparation time: 15 mins

Ingredients

- 20 ounces crabsticks, sliced into thin strips
- 2 tsps. sesame oil
- 1 tsp. Cajun seasoning

Instructions:

Season the crabsticks with some Cajun seasoning and sesame oil.

Cook it in the air fryer at 320°F for 10-12 minutes

Nutrition facts:

Calorie 104.0

Fats 4.5g

Fiber 5.2g

Carbs 14.6g

Protein 4.9g

23.   Sausage Balls

Preparation time: 30 mins

Ingredients

- 1 tsp. sage
- 3 tbsp. breadcrumbs
- ¼ tsp. salt
- 3 ½ ounces sausage meat
- 1 onion, diced
- ½ tsp. garlic powder
- 1/8 tsp. black pepper

Instructions:

Mix all the **Ingredients** in the bowl.

Take about 2-3 tbsp. of the mixture and roll it into a ball in between your palms.

Do the same for the rest of the mixture.

Cook the meatballs in a preheated air fryer at 350°F for 15-20 minutes.

Nutrition facts:

Calorie 65.8

Fats 2.5g

Fiber 0g

Carbs 6.3g

Protein 4.5g

Seafoods

24. <u>**Air Fried Dragon Shrimp**</u>

Preparation time: 15mins

Ingredients

- 1 lb. raw shrimp, peeled and deveined
- 2 eggs 2 tbsp. olive oil
- ½ cup soy sauce
- 1 cup yellow onion, diced
- ½ tsps. ground ginger
- ½ tsps. salt
- ¼ cup flour
- ½ tsps. ground red pepper

Instructions

- Preheat air fryer to 350 degrees F.
- Combine all **Ingredients**, except for the shrimp, and create a batter. Let sit for 10 minutes.
- Dip the shrimp into the batter to coat all sides and place in the fryer basket.
- Cook for 10 minutes and serve.

Nutrition facts:

Calorie 221

Fats 13g

Fiber 0.06g

Carbs 1g

Protein 23g

25.   Air Fryer Keto Shrimp Scampi

Preparation time: 15 mins

Ingredients

- 1 tablespoon chopped chives or 1 teaspoon dried chives
- 1 tablespoon minced basil leaves plus more for sprinkling or 1 teaspoon dried basil
- 2 tablespoons chicken stock (or white wine)
- 4 tablespoons butter
- 1 tablespoon lemon juice
- 1 tablespoon minced garlic
- 2 teaspoons red pepper flakes
- 1 lb. defrosted shrimp (21-25 count)

Instructions

- Turn your air fryer to 330F. Place a 6 x 3 metal pan in it and allow the oven to start heating while you gather your **Ingredients**.
- Place the butter, garlic, and red pepper flakes into the hot 6-inch pan.
- Allow it to cook for 2 minutes, stirring once, until the butter has melted. Do not skip this step. This is what infuses garlic into the butter, which is what makes it all taste so good.
- Open the air fryer, add all **Ingredients** to the pan in the order listed, stirring gently.
- Allow shrimp to cook for 5 minutes, stirring once. At this point, the butter should be well-melted and liquid, bathing the shrimp in spiced goodness.
- Mix very well, remove the 6-inch pan using silicone mitts, and let it rest for 1 minute on the counter. You're doing this so that you let the shrimp cook in the residual heat, rather than letting it accidentally overcook and get rubbery.
- Stir at the end of the minute. The shrimp should be well-cooked at this point.
- Sprinkle additional fresh basil leaves and enjoy.

Nutrition facts:

Calorie 219

Fats 14g

Fiber 0.4g

Carbs 1g

Protein 26g

26. Fish Lettuce Wraps

Preparation time: 20mins

Ingredients

- 6 iceberg lettuce leaves
- 6 small filets of tilapia
- 1 tsp. salt
- ½ tsp. ground black pepper
- 2 tsp. Cajun seasoning
- 1 tbsp. olive oil
- ½ cup shredded purple cabbage
- ½ cup shredded carrot
- 1 tbsp. lemon juice

Instructions

- Preheat the air fryer to 390 degrees F.
- Season tilapia with salt, pepper and Cajun seasoning.
- Drizzle with olive oil and place in the air fryer.
- Cook for 10 minutes.
- Remove fish from the fryer and place the fish on each lettuce leaf.
- Top with carrots and cabbage.
- Drizzle lemon juice on top

Nutrition facts:

Calorie 180

Fats 7g

Fiber 0g

Carbs 0g

Protein 14g

27. Tuna Risotto

Preparation time: 35mins

Serves: 6

Ingredients

- 4 cups chicken broth, warm
- ¼ cup grated parmesan cheese
- 1 tbsp. olive oil
- 2 cups Arborio rice
- ½ cup yellow onion, minced
- 1 cup peas 2 (4oz) cans tuna, drained
- 1 tsp. ground black pepper

Instructions

- Preheat air fryer to 320.
- Season the tuna and peas with black pepper.
- Place in the air fryer and cook for 10 minutes.
- Meanwhile, heat the oil and add the onion and rice. Cook until lightly browned.
- Add 1 cup of the warm broth, and cook until absorbed.
- Repeat until all the broth is used. Stir in the parmesan, tuna, and peas.

Nutrition facts:

Calorie 553

Fats 40g

Fiber 4g

Carbs 23g

Protein 52g

28. **Tandoori Fish**

Preparation time: 25mins

Ingredients

- 1 whole fish, such as trout
- 1 tbsp. garam Masala seasoning
- 3 tbsp. olive oil
- 8 cloves garlic, minced
- 1 cup papaya, mashed
- 1 tsp. ground turmeric
- ½ tsp. ground cumin
- 1 tbsp. chili powder
- 1 tsp. salt ½ tsp. ground black pepper

Instructions

- Preheat the air fryer to 340 degrees F.
- Slash slits into the sides of the fish.
- Combine all remaining **Ingredients** and coat all sides of the fish with the mixture.
- Place the coated fish into the fryer basket and cook for 20 minutes.

Nutrition facts:

Calorie 294.2

Fats 11g

Fiber 7.4g

Carbs 21.4g

Meat Recipes

29. **Air Fryer Marinated Steak**

Prep Time: 5 minutes

Cook Time: 10 minutes

Total Time: 15 minutes

Servings: 2

Ingredients

- 2 New York Strip Steaks (mine were about 6-8 oz each) You can use any cut of steak
- 1 tablespoon low-sodium soy sauce This is used to provide liquid to marinate the meat and make it juicy.
- 1 teaspoon liquid smoke or a cap full
- 1 tablespoon mccormick's Grill Mates Montreal Steak Seasoning or Steak Rub (or season to taste) See recipe notes for instructions on how to create your steak rub
- 1/2 tablespoon unsweetened cocoa powder
- Salt and pepper to taste
- Melted butter (optional)

Instructions

- Drizzle the steak with soy sauce and liquid smoke. You can do this inside Ziploc bags if you wish.
- Season the steak with the seasonings.
- Refrigerate for at least a couple of hours, preferably overnight.
- Place the steak in the air fryer. I did not use any oil. Cook two steaks at a time (if the air fryer is the standard size). You can use an accessory grill pan, a layer rack, or the standard air fryer basket.
- Cook for 5 minutes at 370 degrees. After 5 minutes, open the air fryer and examine your steak. Cook time will vary depending on your desired doneness. Use a meat thermometer and cook to 125° F for

rare, 135° F for medium-rare, 145° F for medium, 155° F for medium-well, and 160° F for well done.

- I cooked the steak for an additional 2 minutes for medium-done steak.
- Remove the steak from the air fryer and drizzle with melted butter.

Nutrition

- Serving: 0.5steak | Calories: 476kcal | Carbohydrates: 1g | Protein: 49g | Fat: 28g

30. **Air Fryer Steak Bites And Mushrooms**

Prep Time: 1 hour 5 minutes

Cook Time: 15 minutes

Total Time: 1 hour 20 minutes

Servings: 2

Ingredients

- 1 teaspoon kosher salt
- 1/2 teaspoon garlic powder
- 1/4 teaspoon black pepper
- 2 Tablespoons Worcestershire Sauce
- 2 Tablespoons avocado oil (Click here for my favorite brand on Amazon)
- 8 oz Baby Bella Mushrooms, sliced
- 1 pound Top Sirloin steak, cut into 1.5 inch cubes

Instructions

- Combine all your ingredients for the marinade into a large mixing bowl.
- Add your steak cubes and sliced mushrooms into your mixing bowl with the marinade and toss to coat.
- Let the steak and mushrooms marinate for 1 hour.
- Preheat your Air Fryer to 400F for 5 minutes.
- Make sure you spray the inside of your air fryer will a cooking spray and pour your steak and mushrooms into the air fryer basket.
- Cook the steak and mushrooms in the Air Fryer for 5 minutes at 400F. Open the basket and shake the steak and mushrooms so they cook evenly. Continue to cook for 5 minutes more.
- Check the steak using an internal meat thermometer. If the steak has not reached your desired doneness, continue to cook in 3-minute intervals until the thermometer placed in the center of 1 steak bite reaches the desired temperature. (Rare=125F, Medium-rare=130F, Medium=140F, Medium-well=150F, well-done=160F)

- Serve

Nutritional Value

- Calories: 572kcal | Carbohydrates: 1g | Protein: 46g | Fat: 43g | Saturated Fat: 22g | Cholesterol: 168mg | Sodium: 219mg | Potassium: 606mg | Sugar: 1g | Calcium: 16mg | Iron: 4mg

31. **Air Fryer Beef Tips**

Prep Time 2 minutes

Cook Time 12 minutes

Marinate Time 5 minutes

Total Time 14 minutes

Servings: 4

Ingredients

- 1 pound ribeye or New York steak, cut into 1-inch cubes
- 2 tsp sea salt
- 1 tsp black pepper
- 1 tsp garlic powder
- 2 tsp onion powder
- 1 tsp paprika
- 2 tsp rosemary crushed
- 2 tbsp coconut aminos

Instructions

- Place steak cubes in a medium sized bowl.
- In a small bowl, combine the salt, pepper, garlic powder, onion powder, paprika, and rosemary. Mix well.
- Sprinkle the mixed dry seasoning on the steak cubes. Mix to evenly distribute the seasoning.
- Sprinkle the coconut aminos all over the seasoned steak. Mix well.
- Let it sit for 5 minutes.
- Place the steak in a single layer in the air fryer basket.
- Cook at 380F for 12 minutes.
- Shake the basket halfway to ensure that the steak cooks evenly.
- Remove from the air fryer and let it cool for a few minutes before serving.

Nutritional Value

- Total fat: 3.7g
- sodium: 1820.8mg
- sugar: 11.3g
- Vitamin A: 169.2ug
- Carbohydrates: 33.6mg
- Protein:18g
- Vitamin C: 165.5mg

32. Air Fryer Beef Kabobs

Prep Time: 30 minutes

Cook Time: 8 minutes

Servings: 4 servings

Ingredients

- 1.5 pounds sirloin steak cut into 1-inch chunks
- 1 large bell pepper color of choice
- 1 large red onion or onion of choice

For The Marinade:

- 4 tablespoons olive oil
- 2 cloves garlic minced
- 1 tablespoon lemon juice
- 1/2 teaspoon
- 1/2 teaspoon
- Salt and pepper pinch

Instructions

- In a large bowl, combine the beef and ingredients for the marinade until fully combined. Cover and marinate in the fridge for 30 minutes or up to 24 hours.
- When ready to cook, preheat the air fryer to 400F. Thread the beef, pepper, and onion onto skewers.
- Place skewers into the preheated air fryer and the air fryer for 8-10 minutes, turning halfway through until charred on the outside and tender on the inside.

Nutrition

Calories: 382kcal | Carbohydrates: 6g | Protein: 38g | Fat: 22g | Saturated Fat: 5g | Cholesterol: 104mg | Sodium: 105mg | Potassium: 708mg | Fiber: 1g | Sugar: 3g | Vitamin A: 1358IU | Vitamin C: 56mg | Calcium: 60mg | Iron:

33. __Air Fryer Corned Beef__

Total Time: 2 hours

Ingredients

- Corned Beef, 3-4 pounds
- 1/2 Cup Brown Sugar
- 1/4 cup Dijon Mustard
- 1 TBSP Apple Cider Vinegar

Instructions

- Mix brown sugar, Dijon mustard, & apple cider vinegar together.
- Baste corned beef with glaze and tightly wrap it in aluminum foil.
- Air Fry at 360 degrees for 1 hour.
- Unwrap aluminum foil, baste again, and loosely wrap with aluminum foil.
- Air Fry at 360 degrees for 40 minutes.
- Remove foil, baste one last time. Air Fry at 400 degrees for 10 minutes.

Nutrition Information:

- Total Fat: 8g|Saturated Fat: 3g|Trans Fat: 0g|Unsaturated Fat: 5g|Cholesterol: 42mg|Sodium: 688mg|Carbohydrates: 16g|Fiber: 0g|Sugar: 15g|Protein: 8g

34. Air Fryer Ground Beef

Prep Time: 2 minutes

Cook Time: 10 minutes

Yield: 6 servings

Ingredients

- 1 to 1 and 1/2 lbs. ground beef
- 1 tsp. salt
- 1/2 tsp. pepper
- 1/2 tsp. garlic powder

Instructions

- Put the ground beef into the basket of the air fryer.
- Season the beef with salt, pepper, and garlic powder. Stir it a bit with a wooden spoon.
- Cook in the air fryer at 400°F for 5 minutes. Stir it around.
- Continue to cook until cooked through and no longer pink, 3-5 more minutes.
- Crumble the beef up using a wooden spoon. Remove the basket and discard any fat and liquid left behind. Use the beef in your favorite ground beef recipe.

Nutritional Value

- Total Fat: 7.5g
- Sodium: 437.5mg
- Sugar: 0g
- Vitamin A: 3.1ug
- Carbohydrates: 0.3g
- Protein: 15.1g

35. <u>Air Fryer Steak With Easy Herb Butter</u>

Prep Time: 6 Mins

Cook Time: 9 Mins

Total Time: 15 Mins

Ingredients

- 2 medium steaks about 8 ounces each
- 2 teaspoon salt
- Herb butter
- 1/4 cup butter softened
- 1 clove garlic
- 1/4 teaspoon salt minced
- 1 tablespoon parsley chopped
- Pepper lots, to taste
- Wine pairings
- 2018 adelante pinot noir
- 2017 hushkeeper zinfandel
- 2018 middle jane cabernet sauvignon reserve

Instructions

- Mix butter, garlic, salt, parsley, and pepper together for herb butter.
- Shape into a log. Chill in the fridge. (See notes.)
- Preheat the air fryer for 5 minutes at 400º F. Liberally salt both sides of the steak. Add the steaks and cook for 7-9 minutes for medium-rare.
- Immediately remove from air fryer. Rest 5 minutes.

Nutrition

- Calories: 678kcal
- Carbohydrates: 1g
- Protein: 46g
- Fat: 55g
- Saturated Fat: 29g

- Cholesterol: 199mg
- Sodium: 2938mg
- Potassium: 608mg
- Sugar: 1g
- Vitamin A: 912IU
- Vitamin C: 3mg
- Calcium: 23mg
- Iron: 4mg
- Net Carbs: 1g

36. __Air Fryer Roast Beef__

Prep Time: 5 Minutes

Cook Time: 45 Minutes

Inactive Time: 10 Minutes

Total Time: 1 Hour

Ingredients

- 2 lb beef roast
- 1 tbsp olive oil
- 1 medium onion, (optional)
- 1 tsp salt
- 2 tsp rosemary and thyme, (fresh or dried)

Instructions

- Preheat air fryer to 390°F (200°C).
- Mix sea salt, rosemary, and oil on a plate.
- Pat the beef roast dry with paper towels. Place beef roast on a plate and turn so that the oil-herb mix coats the outside of the beef.
- Seasoned beef roast on a white plate
- If using, peel the onion and cut it in half, place onion halves in the air fryer basket.
- Place beef roast in the air fryer basket.
- Beef roast in the air fryer basket
- Set to air fry beef for 15 minutes.
- When the time is up, change the temperature to 360°F (180°C). Some air fryers require you to turn food during cooking, so check your manual and turn the beef roast over if required (my Philips Viva air fryer doesn't need food to be turned).
- Set the beef to cook for an additional 30 minutes. This should give you medium-rare beef. Though is best to monitor the temperature with a meat thermometer to ensure that it is cooked to your liking. Cook for additional 5-minute intervals if you prefer it more well done.
- Remove roast beef from the air fryer, cover with kitchen foil and

leave to rest for at least ten minutes before serving. This allows the meat to finish cooking and the juices to reabsorb into the meat.

- Carve the roast beef thinly against the grain and serve with roasted or steamed vegetables, wholegrain mustard, and gravy.

Nutrition Information:

- Calories: 212 | Total Fat: 7g | Saturated Fat: 2g | Unsaturated Fat: 0g | Cholesterol: 83mg | Sodium: 282mg | Carbohydrates: 2g | Fiber: 1g | Sugar: 1g | Protein: 33g

Vegetables Recipes

37. <u>Cauliflower Rice</u>

Prep Time: 30 minutes

Ingredients:

- Tofu:½ block tofu
- ½ cup diced onion
- 2 tbsp. soy sauce
- 1 tsp. turmeric
- 1 cup diced carrot
- Cauliflower:3 cups cauliflower rice (pulsed in a food processor)
- 2 tbsp. soy sauce
- ½ cup chopped broccoli
- 2 garlic cloves, minces
- 1-½ tsp. toasted sesame oil
- 1 tbsp. minced ginger
- ½ cup frozen peas
- 1 tbsp. rice vinegar

Instructions:

Preheat the air fryer to 370 degrees F. Crumble the tofu and combine it with all of the tofu ingredients .Place in a baking dish and air fry for 10 minutes. Meanwhile, place all of the cauliflower ingredients in a large bowl. Mix to combine well. Add the cauliflower mixture to the tofu and stir to combine. Cook for 12 minutes.

Nutrition Facts

Calories 137, Carbohydrates 19.7 g, Fat 4 g, Protein 10.2 g

38. Pasta with Roasted Veggies

Prep Time: 25 minutes

Ingredients:

- 1 lb. penne, cooked
- 1 zucchini, sliced
- 1 pepper, sliced
- 1 acorn squash, sliced
- 4 oz. mushrooms, sliced
- ½ cup kalamata olives, pitted and halved
- ¼ cup olive oil
- 1 tsp. Italian seasoning
- 1 cup grape tomatoes, halved
- 3 tbsp. balsamic vinegar
- 2 tbsp. chopped basil
- Salt and pepper, to taste

Instructions:

- Preheat the air fryer to 380 degrees F.
- Combine the pepper, zucchini, squash, mushrooms, and olive oil, in a large bowl. Season with some salt and pepper.
- Air fry the veggies for 15 minutes. In a large bowl, combine the penne, roasted vegetables, olives, tomatoes, Italian seasoning, and vinegar.
- Divide between 6 serving bowls and sprinkle basil.

Nutrition Facts

Calories 391, Carbohydrates 64.4 g, Fat 14.4 g, Protein 9.5 g

39. **Poblano and Tomato Stuffed Squash**

Prep Time: 50 minutes

Ingredients:

- ½ butternut squash
- 6 grape tomatoes, halved
- 1 poblano pepper, cut into strips
- ¼ cup grated mozzarella, optional
- 2 tsp. olive oil divided
- Salt and pepper, to taste

Instructions:

- Preheat the air fryer to 350 degrees F. Meanwhile, cut trim the ends and cut the squash lengthwise.
- You will only need one half for this recipe. Scoop the flash out, so you make room for the filling.
- Brush 1 tsp. oil over the squash. Place in the air fryer and roast for 30 minutes.
- Combine the other teaspoon of olive oil with the tomatoes and poblanos. Season with salt and pepper, to taste.
- Place the peppers and tomatoes into the squash.
- Cook for 15 more minutes.
- If using mozzarella, add it on top of the squash, two minutes before the end.

Nutrition Facts

Calories 98, Carbohydrates 8.2 g, Fat 5.3 g, Protein 4.3 g

40. Spicy Pepper, Sweet Potato Skewers

Prep Time: 20 minutes

4.9 g

Ingredients:

- 1 large sweet potato
- 1 beetroot
- 1 green bell pepper
- 1 tsp. chili flakes
- ¼ tsp. black pepper
- ½ tsp. turmeric
- ¼ tsp. garlic powder
- ¼ tsp. paprika 1 tbsp. olive oil

Instructions:

- Soak 3 to 4 skewers until ready to use.
- Preheat the air fryer to 350 degrees F.
- Peel the veggies and cut them into bite-sized chunks.
- Place the chunks in a bowl along with the remaining ingredients.
- Mix until fully coated. Thread the veggies in this order: potato, pepper, beetroot.
- Place in the air fryer and cook for 15 minutes.

Nutrition Facts

Calories 335, Carbohydrates 49.6 g, Fat 14.3 g, Protein

41. <u>Grilled Tofu Sandwich</u>

Prep Time: 20 minutes

Ingredients:

- 2 slices of bread
- 1 1-inch thick Tofu slice
- ¼ cup red cabbage, shredded
- 2 tsp. olive oil divided¼ tsp. vinegar Salt and pepper, to taste

Instructions:

- Preheat the air fryer to 350 degrees F.
- Place the bread slices and toast for 3 minutes. Set aside.
- Brush the tofu with 1 tsp. oil and place in the basket of your air fryer. grill for 5 minutes on each side.
- Combine the cabbage, remaining oil, and vinegar, and season with salt and pepper.
- Place the tofu on top of one bread slice, place the cabbage over, and top with the other bread slice.

Nutrition Facts

Calories 225.8, Carbohydrates 21.5 g, Fat 30.5 g, Protein 12.3g

42.   Quinoa and Veggie Stuffed Peppers

Prep Time: 16 minutes

Ingredients:

- ¼ cup cooked quinoa
- 1 bell pepper
- ½ tbsp. diced onion
- ½ diced tomato, plus one tomato slice
- ¼ tsp. smoked paprika
- Salt and pepper, to taste1 tsp. olive oil
- ¼ tsp. dried basil

Instructions:

- Preheat the air fryer to 350 degrees F.
- Core and clean the bell pepper to prepare it for stuffing.
- Brush the pepper with half of the olive oil on the outside. In a small bowl, combine all of the other ingredients, except the tomato slice and reserved half-teaspoon olive oil.
- Stuff the pepper with the filling. Top with the tomato slice.
- Brush the tomato slice with the remaining half-teaspoon of olive oil and sprinkle with basil.
- Air fry for 10 minutes.

Nutrition Facts

Calories 190, Carbohydrates 29.6 g, Fat 6.6 g, Protein 5.7 g

43. __Avocado Rolls__

Prep Time: 15 minutes

Ingredients:

- 3 ripe avocados, pitted and peeled
- 10 egg roll wrappers
- 1 tomato, diced
- ¼ tsp. pepper
- ½ tsp. salt

Instructions:

- Place all of the filling ingredients in a bowl.
- Mash with a fork until somewhat smooth. There should be chunks left.
- Divide the feeling between the egg wrappers.
- Wet your finger and brush along the edges, so the wrappers can seal well. Roll and seal the wrappers.
- Arrange them on a baking sheet lined dish, and place in the air fryer.
- Air fry at 350 degrees F, for 5 minutes. Serve with favorite dipping (I recommend a chili one)

Nutrition Facts

Calories 270, Carbohydrates 24.7 g, Fat 18.7 g, Protein 5.8g

44. Simple Air Fried Ravioli

Prep Time: 15 minutes

Ingredients:

- 1 package cheese ravioli
- 2 cup Italian breadcrumbs
- ¼ cup Parmesan cheese
- 1 cup buttermilk
- 1 tsp. olive oil
- ¼ tsp. garlic powder

Instructions:

- Preheat the air fryer to 390 degrees F.
- In a small bowl, combine the breadcrumbs, Parmesan cheese, garlic powder, and olive oil.
- Dip the ravioli in the buttermilk and then coat them with the breadcrumb mixture.
- Line a baking sheet with parchment paper and arrange the ravioli on it.
- Place in the air fryer and cook for 5 minutes.
- Serve the air-fried ravioli with favorite sauce (I used simple marinara jar sauce)

Nutrition Facts

Calories 298.8, Carbohydrates 42.1 g, Fat 8.7 g, Protein 13.4 g

45. <u>Veggie Kebab</u>

Prep Time: 20 minutes

Ingredients:

- 2 tbsp. corn flour
- 2/3 cup canned beans
- 1/3 cup grated carrots
- 2 boiled and mashed potatoes
- ¼ cup chopped fresh mint leaves½ tsp. garam masala powder
- ½ cup paneer
- 1 green chili1-inch piece of fresh ginger
- 3 garlic clovesSalt, to taste

Instructions:

- Soak 12 skewers until ready to use.
- Preheat the air fryer to 390 degrees F.
- Place the beans, carrots, garlic, ginger, chili, paneer, and mint, in a food processor and process until smooth.
- Transfer to a bowl. Add the mashed potatoes, corn flour, some salt, and garam masala powder to the bowl.
- Mix until fully incorporate. Divide the mixture into 12 equal pieces. (Mine were lemon-sized.)Shape each of the pieces around a skewer.
- Air fry the skewers for 10 minutes.

Nutrition Facts

Calories 211, Carbohydrates 25 g, Fat 11.4 g, Protein 8 g

Salad Recipes

46. <u>Air Fryer Buffalo Salmon Salad</u>

Total Time: 30 mins

Ingredients

- 4 Tbsp. unsalted butter
- ¼ cup hot sauce
- 4 Verlasso salmon fillets (about 1 lb.)
- Cooking spray
- 1 large head romaine lettuce, chopped (about 8 cups)
- 1 ear of corn, kernels removed (or ½ cup frozen corn, thawed)
- ½ cup matchstick carrots
- 1 small red onion, thinly sliced
- 1 bell pepper, thinly sliced
- 3 stalks celery, chopped
- ¼ cup blue cheese crumbles
- Ranch or blue cheese dressing for serving, optional
- Additional hot sauce for serving, optional

Directions

- Melt butter in a small saucepan over medium heat. Remove pan from heat and stir in hot sauce.
- Place salmon in a baking pan and pour the sauce over salmon. Let marinate for 20-30 minutes, turning once halfway through.
- Preheat air fryer to 400°F. Lightly spray the fryer basket with cooking spray. Remove salmon from marinade and pat bottom (skin) dry. Place salmon in basket, skin side down, and cook for 7-10 minutes, or until salmon is cooked to desired doneness.
- While salmon is cooking, assemble the salad. Divide the lettuce among four bowls. Top each bowl with corn, carrots, onion, bell pepper, celery, and blue cheese. Place a salmon fillet on top of each salad.
- Drizzle with dressing and additional hot sauce if desired. Enjoy!

Nutrition

- Calories 360| Total Fat 22g|Cholesterol: 100mg| Sodium: 570mg| Total Carbohydrate: 14g| (Dietary: Fiber 5g| Total Sugars: 6g| Protein: 28g

47. <u>**Grilled Romaine Salad**</u>

Prep Time: 15 mins

Cook Time: 10 mins

Servings: 4 servings

Ingredients

- 2 medium heads of romaine lettuce, cut lengthwise into wedges
- Olive oil for brushing the romaine lettuce
- 1/2 cup crumbled or grated cheese (choose your favorite!)
- Lemon wedges for serving and squeezing over salad

For The Dressing

- 2 cloves garlic, crushed or fine mince
- 3 tablespoons olive oil for the dressing
- Zest of 1 fresh lemon
- 2 tablespoons fresh lemon juice
- 1 tablespoon balsamic vinegar
- 1/2 teaspoon dijon mustard
- 1 teaspoon soy sauce (use tamari for gluten free)
- 1 teaspoon brown sugar
- 1/2 teaspoon paprika
- 1/2 teaspoon kosher salt, or to taste
- Black pepper to taste

Instructions

Make The Dressing

- Whisk together the dressing ingredients (garlic, olive oil, lemon zest, lemon juice, balsamic, mustard, soy sauce, brown sugar, paprika, salt, and black pepper). Set aside.
- Heat the grill to medium-high to high heat (depending on the grill's heat intensity). Make sure to scrape the grill grates so they are clean & food won't stick as easily.

- Lightly coat the romaine lettuce heads with oil. Grill the romaine until they're gently cooked and slightly charred.
- Allow grilled romaine to cool. Lay on a serving tray, drizzle dressing on top, and sprinkle with cheese. Serve with lemon wedges and enjoy!

Nutrition

- Calories: 165kcal | Carbohydrates: 4g | Protein: 4g | Fat: 15g | Saturated Fat: 4g | Cholesterol: 15mg | Sodium: 472mg | Potassium: 48mg | Fiber: 1g | Sugar: 2g | Vitamin C: 4mg | Calcium: 109mg | Iron: 0.3mg

48. Air Fryer Sesame Ginger Salmon With Spicy Cucumber Salad

Prep time: 10mins

Cook time: 8mins

Ingredients

- 1/3 cup Annie's Organic Sesame Ginger Vinaigrette
- 1 pound salmon, cut into 4 portions
- 2 hothouse cucumbers, thinly sliced
- 1 jalapeño, thinly sliced
- A handful of fresh mint leaves, chopped
- 1/2 cup seasoned rice vinegar
- 1/2 teaspoon salt
- 1 teaspoon sugar

Method

- Pour ¼ cup Annie's Sesame Ginger Vinaigrette into the bottom of a medium bowl or baking dish
- Marinate salmon portions skin side facing up in dish for 5 minutes
- Mix cucumber slices, hot pepper, mint, vinegar, salt, + sugar in a large mason jar or medium bowl. Chill cucumber salad in the refrigerator, stirring every 5 minutes while salmon is cooking.
- After salmon has marinated for 5 minutes, place skin side down in air fryer
- Air Fry at 400°F for 8 minutes
- Drizzle salmon with remaining vinaigrette and air fry an additional 1-2 minutes until cooked through, browned, and crispy on the edges
- Using a slotted spoon to eliminate excess pickling juices, place ¼ cucumber salad topped with 1 salmon portion on each plate. Serve immediately!

Nutrient Value

- Calories: 122| Fat: 8g| Sat fat: 2g| Unsatfat: 5g| Protein: 10g|

Carbohydrate| 0g Fiber 0g| Sugars 0g| Added sugars: 0g| Sodium: 254mg

49. Citrus & Avocado Salad

Prep Time: 10 Mins

Total Time: 10 minutes

Ingredients

- 1/2 red grapefruit
- 1 blood orange
- 1 Navel orange
- 1/2 avocado
- 1/4 cup chopped roasted pistachios
- 2 Tbsp. chives
- 1 Tbsp. blood orange infused olive oil
- Sea salt & black pepper to taste!

Instructions

- Slice all citrus in whole circular thin slices.
- Arrange citrus on a large plate and top with avocado slices.
- Garnish with chopped chives, pistachios, blood orange olive oil, sea salt, and pepper.

Nutrient Value

- Total Fat: 22g| Saturated Fat: 10g| Trans Fat: 0g| Unsaturated Fat: 12g| Cholesterol: 88mg| Sodium: 789mg| Carbohydrates: 2g| Fiber: 1g| Sugar: 0g| Protein: 29g

50. <u>Radicchio Salad With Cashew Ricotta Dressing</u>

Prep Time: 10 Minutes

Cook Time: 20 Minutes

Total Time: 30 Minutes

Dressing

- 1/2 cup raw cashews, soaked in hot water for 10 minutes (or sub unroasted macadamia nuts)
- 2 cloves garlic
- 2 Tbsp lemon juice
- 1 ½ Tbsp nutritional yeast
- 1/3 tsp sea salt, plus more to taste
- 1 dash onion powder (optional)
- Water to thin

Beets

- 1 medium beet, thinly sliced into rounds
- 7 cloves garlic, peeled + roughly chopped
- 1 tsp avocado oil (if oil-free, sub maple syrup)
- 1 healthy pinch of each sea salt and black pepper

Candied Walnuts

- 2/3 cup raw walnuts
- 2 tsp maple syrup
- 1 ½ tsp coconut sugar
- 1 pinch sea salt
- 1 dash ground cinnamon

Salad

- 1 head radicchio, rinsed, dried, bottom trimmed, unpeeled, and roughly chopped (~6 cups as the recipe is written)

78

- 1/2 medium lemon, juiced
- 1 healthy pinch of each sea salt and black pepper
- 1/2 cup chopped fresh parsley

Instructions

- Heat oven to 425 degrees F (218 C) and line a baking sheet with parchment paper.
- Add cashews to a small bowl and cover with very hot water. Soak for 10 minutes.
- Add sliced beets and chopped garlic to the prepared baking pan and toss in a bit of oil and salt and pepper. Roast for 10-15 minutes, or until the beets are caramelized and the garlic is golden brown (being careful not to burn).
- In the meantime, add walnuts to a skillet (we prefer cast iron) and heat over medium heat to toast for 5 minutes, stirring frequently, being careful not to burn. Then add maple syrup, coconut sugar, salt, and cinnamon and toss to combine. Turn off heat and allow to cool in the pan.
- In the meantime, prepare the dressing. Drain cashews and add to a small blender (we use this small spice grinder that also has a cup for blending small-batch sauces) along with other dressing ingredients.
- Taste and adjust flavor as needed, adding more garlic for zing, lemon for acidity, salt to taste, or nutritional yeast for cheesiness. It should be zingy, salty, and lemony with a bit of cheesiness. It needs to be quite flavorful, so don't be shy!
- Add radicchio to a serving bowl or platter and toss with lemon juice, salt, and pepper. Then add cashew dressing and toss to coat.
- Top with roasted beets, garlic, and candied walnuts. Garnish with fresh parsley. Serve.

Nutrition Value

- Calories: 274
- Carbohydrates: 20.4 g
- Protein: 9 g
- Fat: 19.6 g
- Saturated Fat: 2.5 g
- Polyunsaturated Fat: 9.44 g

- Monounsaturated Fat: 6.2 g
- Trans Fat: 0 g
- Cholesterol: 0 mg
- Sodium: 286 mg
- Potassium: 579 mg
- Fiber: 4 g
- Sugar: 7.1 g
- Vitamin A: 660 IU
- Vitamin C: 23.46 mg
- Calcium: 67.4 mg
- Iron: 2.82 mg

51. Air Fryer Croutons

Total Time: 30 mins

Ingredients

- 4 slices bread
- 2 tablespoons melted butter
- 1 teaspoon parsley
- 1/2 teaspoon onion powder
- 1/2 teaspoon seasoned salt
- 1/2 teaspoon garlic salt

Instructions

- Preheat the air fryer to 390 degrees.
- Cut 4 slices of bread into bite-sized pieces.
- Melt butter, and place butter into a medium-sized bowl.
- Add 1 teaspoon parsley, 1/2 teaspoon seasoned salt, 1/2 teaspoon garlic salt, 1/2 teaspoon of onion powder to the melted butter. Stir well.
- Add bread to the bowl and carefully stir to coat the bread so that it is coated by the seasoned butter.
- Place buttered bread into the air fryer basket.
- Cook for 5 to 7 minutes or until the bread is toasted.
- Serve immediately.

Nutrition Value

- Calories: 127kcal | Carbohydrates: 14g | Protein: 3g | Fat: 7g | Saturated Fat: 4g | Cholesterol: 15mg | Sodium: 777mg | Potassium: 51mg | Fiber: 1g | Sugar: 2g | Vitamin A: 175IU | Calcium: 39mg | Iron: 1mg

52. __Instant Pot Southern-Style Potato Salad__

Prep Time: 15 minutes

Cook Time: 4 minutes

Chill Time: 1 hour

Total Time 1 hour 19 minutes

Ingredients

- 1 1/2 cups water
- 5 (about 2 pounds total) russet potatoes peeled and sliced into 1 1/2 inch cubes
- 4 eggs
- 1 large bowl of cold water ice added to the water is optional
- 1 cup mayo
- 1/2 cup white onions chopped
- 1/4 cup pickle relish
- 1 tablespoon yellow mustard
- salt and pepper to taste
- Lawry's seasoning salt to taste optional
- 1 teaspoon paprika

Instructions

- Add the water to the Instant Pot. Place the Instant Pot on the saute' function. This will allow the water to warm so that it comes to pressure sooner.
- While the water heats up slice the potatoes.
- Add the steamer basket to the pot. Place the potatoes on top of the basket. Season the potatoes with about 1/4 teaspoon of salt.
- Place the eggs on the very top of the potatoes.
- Close the pot and seal. Cook for 4 minutes on Manual > High-Pressure Cooking.
- When the Instant Pot indicates it has finished cooking, quick release the steam.
- Remove the eggs and place them in the bowl of cold water for 5

minutes.
- Remove the potatoes and transfer to a large bowl.
- Peel the eggs and slice them into small cubes.
- Add the cooked eggs, mayo, mustard, relish, white onions, paprika, and salt and pepper to taste to the mixture. Taste repeatedly. You may need to add additional salt and pepper.
- (If you prefer sweet potato salad add a little more relish and maybe sugar.)
- Stir to combine.
- Cover and chill for at least an hour to two hours before serving.

Nutrition Value

- Calories: 247kcal | Carbohydrates: 13g | Protein: 4g | Fat: 20g

53. <u>Grilled Romaine Salad</u>

Prep Time: 10 Minutes

Cook Time: 2 Minutes

Total Time: 12 Minutes

Ingredients

- 2 heads of romaine lettuce
- 6 slices of bacon
- 6 oz. pomegranate seeds
- 6 oz. of blue cheese crumbles
- 12 oz. of blue cheese dressing (see recipe card below)
- 4 tbsp of olive oil
- 1 tbsp balsamic glaze

Instructions

- Cook the bacon in an air fryer at 370°F for 8-12 minutes until crispy and slice into crumbles. Check out the recipe for the best air fryer bacon.
- Slice the heads of romaine in half, lengthwise.
- Brush the romaine lettuce with olive oil.
- Place the romaine cut side down on the medium-hot grill.
- Flip the heads of romaine after 1-2 minutes and cook on for equal time on the other side.
- Transfer the romaine cut side up to a serving platter and pile on the bacon, pomegranate seeds, and blue cheese crumbles.
- Finish by drizzling the amazing blue cheese salad dressing over the grilled romaine (see recipe below)
- Drizzle with a sweet balsamic glaze, and serve.

Nutrition Information

- Total Fat: 51g
- Saturated Fat: 13g
- Trans Fat: 1g

- Unsaturated Fat: 36g
- Cholesterol: 50mg
- Sodium: 901mg
- Carbohydrates: 17g
- Fiber: 6g
- Sugar: 10g
- Protein: 14g

Dessert And Snacks Recipes

54. <u>Hilton DoubleTree Hotel Chocolate Chip Cookies</u>

Prep Time: 10 mins

Cook Time: 1 hr

Ingredients

- 1/2 cup butter softened
- 1/3 cup granulated sugar
- 1/4 cup packed brown sugar
- 1 egg
- 1/2 teaspoons vanilla extract
- 1/8 teaspoon lemon juice
- 1 cup and 2 tablespoons all-purpose flour
- 1/4 cup rolled oats
- 1/2 teaspoon baking soda
- 1/2 teaspoon salt
- Pinch cinnamon
- 1 1/4 cup semi-sweet chocolate chips
- 1 cup chopped walnuts

Instructions

- Cream butter, sugar, and brown sugar in the bowl of a stand mixer on medium speed for about 2 minutes.
- Add eggs, vanilla, and lemon juice, blending with mixer on low speed for 30 seconds, then medium speed for about 2 minutes, or until light and fluffy, scraping down bowl.
- With the mixer on low speed, add flour, oats, baking soda, salt, and cinnamon, blending for about 45 seconds. Don't overmix.
- Remove bowl from mixer and stir in chocolate chips and walnuts.

- Line the fryer basket with a grill mat or a sheet of parchment paper.
- Scoop about one tablespoon of dough onto a baking sheet lined with parchment paper about 2 inches apart.
- Air fry at 260F (130C) for 18-20 minutes.
- Remove from the air fryer and cool on a wired rack for about 1/2 hour.

Nutrition

- Calories:397kcal| Carbohydrates: 30g | Protein: 5g | Fat: 29g | Saturated Fat: 15g | Cholesterol: 55mg | Sodium: 154mg | Potassium: 182mg | Fiber: 3g | Sugar: 17g | Vitamin C: 1mg | Calcium: 34mg | Iron: 2mg

55. **Hotteok Korean Sweet Pancakes**

Prep Time: 2 hrs 30 mins

Cook Time: 10 mins

Ingredients For The Dough:

- 1 1/4 cup all-purpose flour
- 1/2 tsp salt
- 1 tsp white sugar
- 1 tsp instant dry yeast
- 1/2 cup lukewarm milk
- Ingredients for the filling:
- 1/4 cup brown sugar
- 1/4 tsp cinnamon powder
- 1/4 cup chopped walnuts

Instructions

- In a mixing bowl, mix all the dough ingredients with a spatula.
- Lightly cover the bowl with saran wrap and let the dough rise for about 1-2 hours or until the dough doubles in size.
- Punch the dough down several times to release the air in the dough. Then, cover with saran wrap again and let it rest for about 20 minutes.
- In the meantime, mix all the filling ingredients in a bowl and set aside.
- Line the fryer basket with a grill mat or a sheet of lightly greased aluminum foil.
- Rub some cooking oil in your hands and take the dough out from the bowl. Roll the dough into a cylinder shape on the counter surface then cut it into six equal pieces. Roll each piece into a ball.
- Take one ball of dough and flatten it between the palms of your hand. Scoop about 1 tablespoon of filling and wrap it inside the dough. Place the dough inside the fryer basket, leaving about 2 inches between the balls. Repeat until done.
- Press the balls down with the palm of your hand. Spritz some oil on top and air fry at 300F (150C) for 8-10 minutes, flip once in the middle until the surface is golden brown.

Nutrition

- Calories: 137kcal | Carbohydrates: 24g | Protein: 4g | Fat: 3g | Saturated Fat: 1g | Cholesterol: 2mg | Sodium: 155mg | Potassium: 81mg | Fiber: 1g | Sugar: 8g | Calcium: 29mg | Iron: 1mg

56. Cinnamon Pear Slices

Prep Time: 5 mins

Cook Time: 15 mins

Ingredients

1 medium-sized Asian pear peeled and cored

2 tbsp butter melted

1 tbsp brown sugar

1/2 tsp cinnamon

Granola for garnish optional

Instructions

- Thinly cut the pear into 1/4 inch thick wedges.
- In a mixing bowl, combine and toss all the ingredients.
- Lightly grease a shallow baking pan. Place the pear wedges in the pan, pour whatever is left in the bowl over the pear, and air fry at 340F (170C) for 14-16 minutes until tender.
- Pair them with ice cream or sprinkle some granola over them to serve.

Nutrition

- Calories: 175kcal | Carbohydrates: 20g | Protein: 1g | Fat: 11g | Saturated Fat: 7g | Cholesterol: 30mg | Sodium: 4mg | Potassium: 103mg | Fiber: 3g | Sugar: 15g | Vitamin C: 4mg | Calcium: 8mg | Iron: 1mg

57. Rice Cake Spring Rolls

Prep Time: 10 mins

Cook Time: 10 mins

Ingredients

- Spring roll wrapper
- Chinese sweet rice cake
- A small bowl of water
- Melted butter

Instructions

- Cut the rice cake into rectangles, about 1/4 inch thick.
- Cut the spring roll wrappers to the appropriate size, enough to wrap around the rice cake.
- Wrap the rice cake with spring roll paper. Smear a little water at the end of the wrapper so the wrapper will stick onto itself.
- Line the fryer basket with a grill mat or a sheet of lightly greased aluminum foil.
- Place the wrapped rice cake inside the fryer basket. Brush melted butter onto the wraps and air fry at 400F (2000C) for about 4-5 minutes.
- Flip the rolls over and brush them with butter again. Air fry again at 400F (200C) for another 4-5 minutes until the surface looks crispy and golden brown.
- Let cool about 5 minutes before serving.

58. Candied Kumquats

Prep Time: 5 mins

Cook Time: 10 mins

Ingredients

- 2 cup kumquat
- 2 tbsp melted unsalted butter
- 1/4 cup brown sugar or to taste depending on the sweetness

Instructions

- Cut kumquats in half and pick out all the visible seeds. (Kumquat seeds are edible, therefore it is okay if the seeds cannot be removed completely.)
- In a large mixing bowl, gently stir and mix all the ingredients. Then, transfer the kumquats to a lightly greased bakeware.
- Air fry at 300F (150C) for 10-12 minutes, stirring a couple of times in the middle until there is a slightly thickened sauce.

Nutrition

- Calories: 143kcal | Carbohydrates: 22g | Protein: 1g | Fat: 6g | Saturated Fat: 4g | Cholesterol: 15mg | Sodium: 10mg | Potassium: 123mg | Fiber: 4g | Sugar: 19g | Vitamin C: 25mg | Calcium: 46mg | Iron: 1mg

59. __Pastry Wrapped Rice Cakes__

Prep Time: 10 mins

Cook Time: 10 mins

Ingredients

- Chinese rice cake (nian-ago)
- Pie crust or puff pastry
- Egg wash

Instructions

- Line the fryer basket with lightly greased aluminum foil.
- Cut rice cake into 1/2 inch thick pieces. Wrap the rice cake with pie crust or puff pastry. Lightly press down on the overlapping pie crust to prevent it from opening up. Then, place them in the fryer basket.
- Brush the top side with egg wash. Air fry at 350F (175C) for 4 minutes.
- Flip the rice cake over and brush with egg wash. Air fry again at 350F (175C) for another 4-5 minutes until the surface is golden brown.
- The rice cake hardens when they are cold, so it is best to serve them warm.

Nutrient Value

- Calories: 384kcal | Carbohydrates: 58g | Protein: 16g | Fat: 12g | Saturated Fat: 2g | Sodium: 44mg | Potassium: 737mg | Fiber: 15g | Sugar: 12g | | Vitamin C: 45mg | Calcium: 127mg | Iron: 6mg

60.   **Peanut Butter Cupcake Swirl**

Prep Time: 10 mins

Cook Time: 15 mins

Ingredients

- 1/4 cup butter softened
- 1/3 cup creamy peanut butter
- 2 tbsp sugar
- 1 egg
- 3/4 cup milk
- 1/2 tsp vanilla extract
- 3/4 cup cake flour
- 1 tsp baking soda
- 1/2 tsp baking powder
- 1/2 tsp salt
- 1/4 cup Nutella divided warmed

Instructions

- Line the muffin tins with cupcake liners and set them aside.
- Cream together the butter, sugar, and peanut butter using a whisk or an electric mixer. Then, add the egg, milk, and vanilla extract. Mix until homogenous. Finally, add the rest of the dry ingredients and mix until well combined.
- Scoop the batter into the liners about 2/3 full. Then, use a spoon to drop about 1/2 teaspoon of Nutella into the center of the cupcake. Insert a toothpick into the center of the Nutella and create a swirl by making circles in the batter.
- Air fry at 300F (150C) for about 12-14 minutes. Insert a toothpick to test. When the toothpick comes out clean, then the cupcake is cooked through.

Nutrition

- Calories: 215kcal | Carbohydrates: 18g | Protein: 5g | Fat: 14g | Saturated Fat: 7g | Cholesterol: 34mg | Sodium: 378mg |

94

CPSIA information can be obtained
at www.ICGtesting.com
Printed in the USA
BVHW090821030621
608729BV00003B/1004